THE
A B C
OF
CULTS

D1549780

THE
A B C
OF
CULTS

Bryan Williams

Christian Focus

© Bryan Williams
ISBN 1 85792 248 4
Published in 1997
by
Christian Focus Publications,
Geanies House, Fearn, Ross-shire,
IV20 1TW, Great Britain

Contents

PREFACE 7

ATONEMENT MISUNDERSTOOD 11

BIBLE SUPPLEMENTED 12

CHRISTOLOGICAL ERROR 13

DILUTION OF SCRIPTURE 14

EMOTIONAL CAPTIVITY 15

FINANCIAL MANIPULATION 16

GOD MISREPRESENTED 17

HIDDEN AGENDAS 18

INTROVERTED TEACHING 20

JESUS DOWNGRADED 21

KARMA 22

LEGALISM 24

MESSIANIC CLAIMS 26

NEPOTISM 27

OPPRESSIVE LEADERSHIP 28

PERVASIVE SECRECY 29

QUIRKY TEACHING 30

REJECTION OF OUTSIDERS 31

SYNCRETISM 33

TIMES CONFUSED 35

UNBALANCED EMPHASIS 36

VEDANTIST TEACHING 37

WORKS 39

XTIANITY REVILED 40

YOUTHFUL INDOCTRINATION 41

ZODIACAL ASTROLOGY 43

PREFACE

What is a cult? How may it be recognised? Why are the so-called main-line churches not described as cults? In this little book we are seeking to answer these and similar questions. An attempt is made to give an overall picture of what a cult is, and to point out the major differences between cults and true churches.

The method of treatment includes a positive statement of what the Bible teaches about a subject, along with a selection of supportive biblical texts. Key features of cults are listed alphabetically. We note particular cults and their characteristics. Usually three or four different cults – ancient or modern, eastern or western – surface in each entry.

Often the word 'cult' is used very loosely. It frequently means any way-out or eccentric community. Television producers love to weave some fictional story around strange groups on the fringes of society!

In this little book we are not thinking quite like that. We are seeking more precision. We are considering cults from a Christian point of view. *A cult is a system or an organisation that*

7

differs from the Bible's portrayal of Christianity in important areas of teaching, behaviour, and/or ritual.

Usually claims are advanced by cultic groups suggesting supposed refinements or updates of the Christian Faith. Accordingly, some movements take pride in their alleged ability to 'improve' on the Faith once delivered to the saints. Other movements cut adrift from the Gospel altogether, and, with or without assistance from existing non-Christian organisations, launch out in new directions.

In contrast with such false systems stands the Church, the Body of Christ, which will finally consist of all spiritually reborn people, whether they are already in heaven or still upon the earth, not yet converted or even not yet born. Within this 'great multitude that no one could count' (Revelation 7:9) there is the present Church on earth, visible in hundreds of denominations and tens of thousands of congregations.

Obviously there are many respects in which one church or group differs from another, but in our definition above we stress the words, 'important areas'. It is serious deviations that we have in mind when we speak of cults, not things like how often a church celebrates Communion, or exactly what model of church government it favours, or what view of the Millennium it holds. Some such issues are unimportant, while others have a degree of importance, but are not presented with absolute clarity in the Bible. It is truly central biblical issues like the Godhood of our Lord Jesus Christ, the view of mankind, the real nature of the human predicament, and the way of salvation that distinguish the orthodox Christian from the adherent of the cult.

Cults exibit endless variations. There are hundreds, perhaps thousands, of different systems: someone has counted 2500 in the United States alone! To describe them in detail would be a colossal task. In many respects it would also be an unprofitable one. It is certainly easier, as well as being altogether more helpful to the Christian, to set out only the recurring features of cultic groups and beliefs. Not all the features in our 'alphabet' are found in all cults. Still, the characteristics listed appear again and again in the ever-changing patterns of weird movements. Nearly all the features are really significant deviations from the true Faith of the Bible, the only possible exceptions being 'N', 'R', 'T' and 'U'.

ATONEMENT MISUNDERSTOOD

The Bible teaches that atonement for sinful human beings begins with the grace of God. Atonement is realised by grace *alone*, with no input whatsoever from man's side (Ephesians 2:1-8). God's grace is expressed most clearly in the death of the Lord Jesus Christ. The Lord Jesus Christ died voluntarily, and that for others (John 10:14-18). His substitutionary death effectively deals with sin as the Holy Spirit mysteriously grants new birth (John 3:1-8). God demands that we act responsively: 'Repent and believe the good news!' (Mark 1:15, Acts 2:36-47).

Contrary views come from Jehovah's Witnesses (Christ's death gives man a chance to earn salvation), Christian Scientists (salvation is from ignorance about the non-reality of matter and not from sin), and the New Apostolics (salvation comes through baptism and 'holy sealing', both necessarily performed by New Apostolic 'apostles'). Together with errors about the Person of our Lord Jesus Christ, errors about the Atonement are the most central and serious of all cultic errors.

BIBLE SUPPLEMENTED

The Bible, consisting of the Old and New Testaments, has for centuries been recognised by Christendom as the Word of God – trustworthy as God is trustworthy. It is true that problems have long been around concerning the validity of the Apocrypha, but that addition to Scripture shows its illegitimacy by its inconsistency in vital aspects with the books universally accepted by the Church. God's Word is true (John 17:17), and indeed flawless (Psalm 18:30). Certain cults *add* to Scripture, and always add contrary material. The Mormons claim extra revelations. The Moonies' book *Divine Principle* is another alleged supplement to the Bible.

On the other hand, there are those who *reduce* the Bible for their own ends. In ancient times the Samaritans did so, and so did the Sadducees. In the last two centuries especially fierce battles have raged over the list of true biblical books. Numerous liberal Protestants have narrowed the range to suit their own preferences. Many have gone further ... while still calling themselves Christians they have rejected the idea of God-given authoritative books altogether! In the spirit of the age, they have tried to shrug off all authority.

CHRISTOLOGICAL ERROR

This is the fountainhead of all cultic aberrations! When people are blind to the nature of the glorious Son of God, all manner of other false teachings follow. The Bible teaches that Jesus Christ is eternal (John 1:1,2, 17:5). He is God (John 20:28, Hebrews 1:8). He is also man (John 8:40, Romans 1:1-4). He is neither of these separately, but was and is a perfectly unified Person (John 1:14). He is entirely free from the taint of sin (1 Peter 1:18,19, 1 John 3:4,5). He is Prophet (Hebrews 1:1,2), Priest (Hebrews 4:14-16) and King (Revelation 19:11-16). He is the Agent of creation (John 1:1-3) and the one who actually keeps all things in existence (Colossians 1:15-17).

It is hard to know where to begin in naming cults with serious christological errors. Here we'll mention only three or four. Undoubtedly the most influential group to consider is the Protestant Liberal camp again. There are almost as many different views of Christ as there are Liberals. Besides that, there have been at least two major 'waves' of opinion over the last one hundred years among such people. Still, in all their variety, Liberals deny Christ's Godhood (usually), his eternity (almost always), his sinlessness (sometimes), and even his existence (occasionally). Jehovah's Witnesses teach that Christ was created by the Father and is less than God. So-called Christian Scientists and the 'Unity' School of Christianity have a confused idea of Jesus and Christ as two distinct persons.

DILUTION OF SCRIPTURE

This is not quite the same as the last paragraph under 'B'! Besides those who reject parts of the Bible because they claim that it is no longer relevant – or for some other reason – there are folk who retain the Bible intact but empty it of its power. One way of doing this is by simple neglect, by leaving the Bible on the shelf. The Christian Scientists dilute Scripture by distorting its contents ... they deny the existence of matter as if Genesis 1 had never been written. Christadelphians say that they have no Scriptures but the Bible, but the answers they get from it are a pale shadow of the clear and strong message it really contains. Moral Re-Armament has no creed, no theology, but seems to claim a kind of Christian colouring for its system nonetheless.

EMOTIONAL CAPTIVITY

True Christianity means marvellous freedom. Coming to belong to the family of God through repentance and wholehearted commitment to the Lord Jesus Christ is a matter of emerging from captivity to liberty. Jesus said that if the Son makes people free they are 'free indeed' (John 8:31-36). Romans 8, a gem of a chapter, is largely occupied with this very subject. Paul writes of believers having been transferred from the dominion of darkness to the kingdom of light (Colossians 1:10-14).

An ugly catalogue of movements that have specialised in emotional captivity or psychological bondage could easily be compiled. Such groups have caused revulsion even among non-Christians. They have turned people away from the Faith because the undiscerning have mistaken the counterfeit for the genuine. That has been the exact situation with the cult believed responsible for the nerve gas attacks in the Japanese subways this year or so ago. Buddhists in Japan have asked Christians if they have links with the cult! The 'Unification Church' (Moonies) of Sun Myung Moon has similarly controlled the lives of its adherents, and caused terrible grief to countless individuals and families. Scientology has been perceived as such a threat to mental equilibrium that its leaders have been banned from entering even some Western 'tolerant' countries.

FINANCIAL MANIPULATION

Every now and then the media portray some outlandish group that makes total demands of its followers, requiring them to turn over all possessions to the cult's leaders. Sometimes the demand impoverishes the ordinary members as it enriches those in power. Certain of the Indian gurus with Hindu connections drive round in the most opulent cars and enjoy an extravagant lifestyle, while their devotees are driven to destitution.

The Bible teaches the principle of tithing in the Old Testament (for example, in Malachi 3:10). God commanded the Israelite worshipper to bring a tenth of the grain and farm animals to the priests as God's representatives (Leviticus 27, especially verses 30 to 32). In the New Testament no actual proportion of a person's income is required as a tithe, but Christian giving is to be cheerful, voluntary and generous. Such giving is never intended to make the giver a pauper (2 Corinthians, chapters 8 and 9).

GOD MISREPRESENTED

God is personal, eternal, spiritual and creator of all except himself. God is one, but threefold in nature. Father, Son and Holy Spirit are co-equal in unchanging glory, perfect and complete knowledge, righteousness, holiness, power and love. God is everywhere present throughout the Universe he has made, but is at the same time far above and beyond it, not limited by it. A few biblical references demonstrating these truths are Matthew 6:9-13, 1 Chronicles 16:36, John 4:24, Genesis 1:1, 2:1, James 2:19, 2 Corinthians 13:14, and 1 John

4:8. An exceptional chapter on the character of God is Psalm 139. Job 38 and 39 also portray God's person and capabilities vividly.

Against the Bible's teaching we find all sorts of error assembled. The Mormons say that they believe in the Trinity, but they actually worship three gods, and 'gods' who have flesh at that! Christ is the son of Adam-God and Mary! The 'holy spirit' differs from the spirit of god, they say. Freemasons actually hold to the idea of a composite god under the initials J.B.O.: Jehovah of Israel, Baal of the Canaanites, and On or Osiris of Egypt! Swedenborg was a kind of Unitarian, reviving the ancient heresy of Sabellius. Theosophy and the New Age Movement are pantheistic, holding the theory that God is all, and all is God. None of these views can stand for a moment once the authority of the Bible as the Word of God is recognized and its pages studied.

HIDDEN AGENDAS

Our Lord Jesus Christ told his disciples: 'What I tell you in the dark, speak in the daylight; what is whispered in your ear, proclaim from

18

the roofs' (Matthew 10:27). Later, in the Great Commission, he said that Christians were to go and 'make disciples of all nations' (Matthew 28:19). Even if the Gospel message is at first known to only a handful of Jesus' followers, it is his declared purpose that they should tell it to others. They in turn should tell still others, according to the principle of Titus 1:9: 'He (the elder in this case) must hold firmly to the trustworthy message as it has been taught, so that he can encourage others by sound doctrine and refute those who oppose it.' That the early Christians obeyed the Lord's command is perfectly clear in Acts. We read that after the death of Stephen: 'Those who had been scattered preached the word wherever they went' (8:4).

In the strongest possible contrast, modern groups often revel in secrets that are only gradually revealed, and then exclusively to insiders. The obvious desire is to keep the odd ideas of the cult away from the newcomer for as long as possible, so that he or she may become convinced that the group is actually orthodox or spiritually 'neutral'. Then, when the person is well and truly 'hooked', a more bizarre diet is progressively introduced. Yoga is often presented as a harmless regime of exercises, whereas it is really a 'lead-in' to various types of Hinduism. Transcendental Meditation is also advertised as if it was not a religion, but the occult and Hinduism are not far below the surface.

INTROVERTED TEACHING

Quite simply, this means standing the truth on its head! In the early days of the Church there were strangely perverted groups that made heroes of the evil personages of the Bible and enemies of the good. The Ophites (from the Greek word for snake) worshipped the serpent and reviled God. The Cainites honoured Cain and despised Abel. Modern Satanists do the same sort of thing. Those who indulge in the ancient evil of spiritism in effect follow an identical path. No less dangerous is idolatry, which is essentially worshipping someone or something created rather than the Creator.

The Lord God's condemnation of all such things is devastating and total. Deuteronomy 18:9-13 repeatedly uses the strong word 'de-

testable' to show God's attitude. The Psalmist and Isaiah poke fun at pitiful supposed
'gods' (Psalm 115:4-8, Isaiah 40:18-20). Paul
shows that the evil of idolatry leads straight
on to vile practices (Romans 1:18-32). The
Apostle does not mince words; he often refers
to the 'wrath of God', and the New Testament
confirms in many places that the inevitable end
of all sinful beliefs and acts is hell. (See, for
example, Revelation 21:8). The only way for
any human being to escape the consequences
of these and other sins is to seek Christ in repentance and faith (Acts 4:8-12, Mark 1:15).

JESUS DOWNGRADED

Paul, writing at the bidding of the Holy Spirit,
asserts:

> God exalted him to the highest place and
> gave him *the name that is above every name*,
> that at the name of Jesus every knee should
> bow, in heaven and on earth and under the
> earth, and every tongue confess that Jesus
> Christ is Lord ... (Philippians 2:9-11).

In another letter Paul writes concerning Jesus: *that in everything he might have the supremacy* (Colossians 1:18).

Jesus is belittled by every group that wants to make him less than the Father, or to share his exalted position with counterfeits. Into the first category we must place the Jehovah's Witnesses. They tend to admit that Jesus is God, but only in some secondary fashion since they declare he was created. Hindus and Freemasons share the second category, both conceding that Jesus is ONE of the world's great religious leaders. In principle there is no difference between the two systems regarding Christology – it is just that Hinduism has the doubtful honour of accepting millions more 'gods'!

KARMA

Both Buddhism and Hinduism believe in Karma. The sum total of a person's actions, whether good or bad, is somehow reckoned up in a kind of heavenly register. All actions of all supposed incarnations to date contribute towards the next stage in destiny. According to those who accept karma, there is no possibility whatever of escaping the consequences of one's personal histories. Some cults with Eastern roots but active in the West have adopted the theory of karma: one is Theosophy, and another is the Anthroposophy movement of Rudolf Steiner.

The Bible has nothing to say about karma. It uniformly teaches that we have but one life on earth. Since the fall into sin by our first parents, Adam and Eve, all people are born in a state of condemnation by God. If we do not commit ourselves to Christ we will die in our sins (John 8:24), having nothing to look forward to but judgment and hell (Hebrews 9:27, Revelation 20:11-15). But – and it is a big but – 'now is the time of God's favour, *now is the day of salvation*' (2 Corinthians 6:2). God has graciously provided a way out, a way of salvation. *Jesus* is the way (John 14:6) through his death for sinners (1 Peter 3:18). Total submission, sustained submission, to him in repentance and faith is the path of blessing, true joy, and heaven itself. What applied to the church in Philadelphia applies in every similar situation! Please read Revelation 3:7-13.

LEGALISM

Many Christians think that legalism means being strict and inflexible in standards and conduct. In some contexts perhaps that is a satisfactory definition. Legalism can be 'red tape'. However, theologically speaking, it means *the doctrine of justification by works*. Legalism is the foe of justification by grace alone. It is the denial of the gospel: 'For it is by grace you have been saved, through faith – and this not from yourselves, it is the gift of God – not by works, so that no one can boast' (Ephesians 2:8,9). Paul teaches much about grace in Romans 5, 6 and 9.

Any system that claims we can be justified by works or by Christ plus works is legalistic. The Pharisees in Jesus' day were legalists of the first sort. So are Hindus. Legalists of the second sort include the 'Judaisers' the Apostle Paul opposes in his Epistle to the Galatians. They retained observance of the Old Testament Law (especially circumcision) in addition to faith in the Lord Jesus. Only a combination of the two spelled acceptance with God! Paul is scathing about such ideas in Galatians 3:1-14.

He calls the false teaching 'a different gospel – which is really no gospel at all' (1:6,7). The New Apostolic Church of Germany, England and South Africa is legalistic in the Galatian sense, even though the issue is no longer circumcision. Herbert Armstrong's cult, The World Church of God, has traditionally been legalistic, demanding lawkeeping both for obtaining and retaining salvation. (However, according to an article that appeared in the Winter 1996 issue of *Christian Research Journal*, The Worldwide Church of God has undergone a radical transformation. Under the leadership of Joseph Tkach, the organisation confesses that it was previously in serious error and judgmental, condemning those outside its number. It had called Christians 'deceived' and 'instruments of Satan'. Tkach says that now the The Worldwide Church of God affirms the biblical doctrine of the Trinity and 'the sufficiency of our Lord's substitutionary sacrifice to save us from the death penalty for sin. We teach salvation by grace, based on faith alone, without resort to works of any kind.'

Besides its fatal flaw – it is unscriptural – legalism leaves a person with no assurance whatever. The legalist, like Saul of Tarsus, is ever in emotional turmoil. He or she is always struggling to make greater efforts in order to be acceptable with God. The legalist is forever tormented with the question: 'Have I made the grade?'

MESSIANIC CLAIMS

Blasphemous claims to be the messiah are nothing new! Gamaliel the Pharisee named two before the Church even emerged from its infancy. Theudas and Judas the Galilean must have been messianic pretenders of a kind, because the learned scholar compared the Lord Jesus to them (Acts 5:34-39). Among more modern so-called 'christs' is Joseph Smith of the Mormons, at least in respect of his assertions to be the authoritative revealer of God, though Smith also found room in his system for another christ something like the Jehovah's Witnesses' christ.

Regarding true revelation the Apostle John tells us: 'For the law was given through Moses; grace and truth came through Jesus Christ. No one has ever seen God, but God the One and

Only, who is at the Father's side, has made him known' (John 1:17,18). The true revelation leads straight to the true Christ!

Another 'christ' is Sun Myung Moon of the Unification Church (Moonies). Moon claims that our Lord Jesus Christ did not finish his saving activities, and so a new messiah was necessary. Moon strongly implies that he himself is that messiah: 'I think that of all of God's saints, I am the most successful one'! Yet another 'christ' is Maharaj Ji of the Hindu-type movement called Divine Light Mission. Followers assert that Ji is the most important incarnation of 'God' that ever trod the face of this planet! In Theosophy the Lord Jesus is regarded as the greatest of God's revelations up to the present, but the next 'christ' is supposed to be superior to him!

NEPOTISM

Nepotism means favouritism shown to relatives, especially when influential positions are granted to them. Medieval popes sometimes conferred such favours on their biological children. The origin of the major division of the

Muslims into Sunni and Shiite factions lies in a situation of this kind, the latter viewing relatives of the prophet as the true imams. A breakaway group of Mormons descended from Joseph Smith and so called the 'Josephites' has its headquarters in Missouri.

OPPRESSIVE LEADERSHIP

In a famous passage in the Gospel of Matthew Jesus declares: 'Come to me, all you who are weary and burdened, and I will give you rest. Take my yoke upon you and learn from me, for I am gentle and humble in heart, and you will find rest for your souls. For my yoke is easy and my burden is light' (11:28-30). On our Lord's last evening before the crucifixion he described his disciples as 'friends' rather than 'servants' because of the way he was treating them (John 15:14,15). Earlier he had emphatically told the Twelve that they were not to 'lord' it over one another (Mark 10:35-45).

All of these Scriptures are totally different in tone from that of the leaders of modern cults. Lording it over others is exactly what a lot of them do! More, some cultic bosses actually brainwash their followers. Sun Myung Moon and his cult control the choice of marriage partners for their fellow-cultists. The effect on family life is often calamitous. 'Father' Moon takes the place of Christ, has hymns sung to him, and even claims to forgive sins! Scientology, whose methods were originally called 'Dianetics', involves brainwashing – along with an abandonment of the true teaching of the Word of God.

PERVASIVE SECRECY

There is a subtle difference here from our *Hidden Agendas* entry above. In most cases with the earlier entry the whole teaching is gradually revealed to all adherents of the group, however exalted or lowly they may be in the system. For a marked contrast we can look at Freemasonry. Here secrecy is taken to extreme lengths. Members make themselves known to one another by distinctive handshakes or a code-word. In the secret society a Mason must pass a number of 'degrees' (in Scotland 33; in France only 7) before he gets near the Mystic Shrine. Each member has to take horrifying oaths that he will preserve an absolute silence about what he learns. The penalties for failing to keep vows become more severe with increasing seniority.

To the Biblical verses quoted under *Hidden Agendas* can be added our Lord's statement recorded in Acts 1:8: 'you will be my witnesses in Jerusalem, and in all Judea and in Samaria, and to the ends of the earth.' The openness of testimony to Jesus Christ and his salvation is characteristic of the true Church, and foreign to certain cults.

QUIRKY TEACHING

Sometimes unbiblical teaching may appear merely quaint and comparatively harmless. So it is perhaps with the Seventh Day Adventists and their emphasis on Sabbath keeping. In this instance the issue can be either important or less so. If the people concerned teach that observing Saturday as the Lord's Day is an essential element in salvation, they are guilty of the old heresy of Galatianism. They are making the cross less than the basis of justification by adding to Christ's atonement. We know how strongly Paul condemns *that* in Galatians 1!

However, if the keeping of Saturday is only perceived as something desirable, few would have any serious quarrel with such folk. (As a matter of fact, some SDA's hold one position and some the other, so their orthodoxy is a subject of considerable debate.)

Unmistakeable error, however, is apparent in the denial of the real existence of anything physical by the Christian Scientists, the Unity School of Christianity, and every other type of Gnosticism, whether ancient or modern. Any scheme that so clearly contradicts God's repeated assessment of what he created shares the grievous sin of Satan himself. He rejected the Lord's word outright! See Genesis 1:9,12,18,21,25,31 and 3:3 and 4.

Much more could be said, of course! *Every* movement that qualifies as a cult by opposing the teaching God gives and the practice he commands in Scripture is quirky!

REJECTION OF OUTSIDERS

True Christians may meet for the first time having come from different cultures, different countries, and very different denominations, but they generally still recognise each other as belonging to the Lord. A host of inter-church movements bears eloquent testimony to the underlying oneness – Scripture Union, Youth for Christ, YMCA, YWCA, and the inter-denominational missions like Wycliffe Bible Translators, Overseas Missionary Fellowship, Africa Inland Mission, Africa Evangelical Fellowship and Operation Mobilisation. Even where there is rivalry it very rarely reaches the stage of denying the genuineness of the spiritual experience of another saved by the grace of God.

It is far otherwise with the cults!

The Jehovah's Witnesses dismiss true Christians as being 'of the devil'.

The followers of Joseph Smith say that non-Mormons will be cast into hell unless they repent.

Christadelphians declare orthodox Christianity an abomination of the earth.

The Armstrong sect has branded both Protestantism and Romanism 'pagan'.

Freemasonry says that all Christians outside their fold are in a state of darkness.

The New Apostolic Church teaches that only those 'sealed' by the laying on of hands and baptism can be saved. The rites are only valid when an 'Apostle' performs them.

The reader will not find it difficult to decide which group – the Christians or the cultists – comes closer to the Lord Jesus' expressed desire. Talking of his disciples he says: 'My prayer is not for them alone. I pray also for those who will believe in me through their message, that all of them may be one, Father, just as you are in me and I am in you. May they also be in us so that the world may believe that you have sent me. I have given them the glory that you gave me, that they may be one as we are one: I in them and you in me. May they be brought to complete unity to let the world know that you sent me and have loved them even as you have loved me' (John 17:20-23).

SYNCRETISM

Syncretism is the word for the attempt to unify contradictory beliefs and practices.

The phenomenon is at least as old as the ancient Israelites, who in their worst moments tried to combine worship of Yahweh, the Lord God, with acknowledgment of the immoral Canaanite religion. There are numerous modern equivalents. One is Bahaism, which claims to be the universal religion, and which possesses an imposing temple near Chicago. Nine entrances stand for nine different religions that are all supposed to lead to the one truth. In Africa there are millions of people who try to make an amalgam of Christianity and their traditional religions. Theosophy has adopted elements from Hinduism, Gnosticism, Spiritism, and the Bible. The New Age Movement is a confusing mixture of pantheism, the occult, reincarnation, karma, a change of consciousness, and very much else.

How the clear-cut gospel of our Lord Jesus Christ differs from all these man-made religions! A tiny selection of verses from the Old and New Testaments follows:

You shall have no other gods before me (Exodus 20:3).

Jesus said to him, 'Away from me, Satan! For it is written: "Worship the Lord your God, and serve him only"' (Matthew 4:10).

Salvation is found in no one else, for there is no other name {than that of the Son of God} under heaven given to men by which we must be saved (Acts 4:12).

TIMES CONFUSED

The most commonly confused time is the date of the Second Coming of Christ.

Jesus himself said: 'You...must be ready, because the Son of Man will come at an hour when you do not expect him' (Luke 12:40). At the end of his earthly ministry Jesus revealed many indicators relating to his return to the disciples (see Matthew 24), but only one of them was very precise. In Matthew 24:14 his words are: 'And this gospel of the kingdom *will be preached in the whole world* as a testimony to all nations, and then the end will come.'

Both Christians and cultists have been over-eager in declaring which year, month, day, or even hour our Lord would return, but there is no doubt that the cults have held to their views with more vehemence! Multitudes waited confidently for the Lord to return in the year AD 1000. William Miller, the (unwitting?) founder of the Seventh Day Adventists, predicted that the Second coming would be in 1843. Later he settled for 1844. The Jehovah's Witnesses claim an invisible Second Coming occurred in 1914. The last theory is farcical. Scripture teaches that Jesus will return personally, physically, visibly, audibly, and with splendour (Acts 1:9-11, Revelation 1:7, 1 Thessalonians 4:16).

UNBALANCED EMPHASIS

All Christians are guilty of having a skewed view of things in one way or another. Only God is perfectly balanced in outlook, because only he has complete knowledge, unfettered by either creaturely limitation or sin. For all that, we Christians can and should become more informed as well as more godly as time goes on. Finally our knowledge will be clear and as complete as possible for a finite being (1 Corinthians 13:12 – compare 2 Corinthians 3:18 and 1 John 3:2).

Every group that we scrutinise in this book is unbalanced, to say the least!

Here we look at the British Israelites. They are not strictly a cult at all. Some would say that they are not even an organisation, but just certain Christians wedded to a rather odd idea. Sometimes, perhaps, but there are 'Anglo-Saxon Associations' in some parts of the English-speaking world. British Israelite theory is that Britain is descended from the Israelite tribe of Ephraim and the United States from Manasseh. The theory is so bizarre that it is not surprising that serious Bible scholars have no time for it!

VEDANTIST TEACHING

Of all cults that enjoy wide popularity in the West, the majority come in one of two main categories. There are the 'home-grown' western systems, many of them from the United States, and there are the Eastern systems usually derived in some way from Hinduism. Comparatively few cults trace their origin to Buddhism alone, while Bahaism is the only cult coming from Islam with a large following outside the Muslim world. (Islam itself, of course, like Hinduism, Buddhism, Confucianism, and Marxism, is a cult. Generally, though, these are all regarded as 'world religions', because, while plainly deviant from Christianity, they are hardly derived from it.)

The Vedas are the ancient 'sacred' books of the Hindus. They are in the Sanskrit language, and consist primarily of hymns, prayers and charms. The Hare Krishna movement, also called ISKCON (International Society for Krishna Consciousness) is a Vedic cult. So is the Divine Light Mission of the guru Maharaj Ji. Transcendental Meditation derives from Hindu philosophy as well. One of the characteristics of Hindu religious groups is a readiness to 'add' Jesus Christ to the collection of idolatrous gods already worshipped. Such a practice would have attracted the scorn of the Psalmist (78:56-58), Isaiah (44:9-20) and Paul (Galatians 1:6-9). In Colossians Paul greatly stresses the uniqueness and supremacy of the Lord Jesus Christ over every supposed rival.

WORKS

Paul wrote over and over again that sinful human beings are saved in one way alone: by the grace of God. Christians often quote Romans 3:23 when witnessing, but for present purposes we need to go both a little back and a little forward from that verse to get the full force of the apostle's teaching. With Jews and Gentiles alike in mind he says: 'There is no difference, for all have sinned and fall short of the glory of God, *and are justified freely by his grace through the redemption that came by Christ Jesus.*' In the equally well known Ephesians 2:8,9 the Apostle writes: 'For it is by grace you have been saved, through faith – and this not from yourselves, it is the gift of God – not by works, so that no one can boast.' At the start of Romans 4 Paul says that even Abraham was not counted right in God's sight because of 'works' but through faith. Works, then, whether regarded as 'religious' like circumcision or Sabbath-keeping, or as acts of kindness, are *never* the route to God. Needless to say, our Lord Jesus Christ had taught exactly what Paul did. When some casual followers asked: 'What must we do to do the works God requires?' he took up their word and turned it around! He replied: 'The work of God is this: to *believe* in the one he has sent.'

Cult after cult founders at this point. It is a terrible blow to human pride to think that God will forgive our sins because of what he has done (in Christ) rather than anything we can do!

The Pharisees held that people are accepted by God because of their works. This conviction does not come from the Old Testament, but is accepted in spite of the Old Testament. The Mormons apparently believe in Christ (but which Christ?), but add baptism, good works, and submission to Joseph Smith's instruction before salvation is achieved. The Jehovah's Witnesses, though less unorthodox than the Mormons, also believe in works for salvation. The New Apostolics and Herbert Armstrong's disciples are in the same fundamental camp (but see note under 'L').

XTIANITY REVILED

Perhaps we may be excused for using the theological student's abbreviation for Christianity in order to get our 'X' into the sequence!

Much of what we've said under *Rejection of Outsiders* fits here. Actually in country after country almost any religion is accepted or at least tolerated except *the orthodox Christian Faith*. Even in so-called Christian countries, often especially in them, blasphemy is common in the media, and irreverent fun is poked at Christianity, but woe betide anyone who does the same to Islam or Hinduism! So-called Western Secularism is the worst offender. For instance *Punch* magazine for a time regularly included particularly vicious cartoons attacking Christianity. Similarly, American and European pagan anthropologists have mounted a sustained attack against true missionary work, pretending that the Lord's people are destroying 'noble' heathen cultures, and conveniently ignoring all the ugly features of both those cultures and of the degenerate western anti-Christian culture.

YOUTHFUL INDOCTRINATION

Indoctrination often just means to teach someone a series of related facts. It is then a 'neutral' matter spiritually and morally, with no emotional undertones. A second significance attaches to the word, though. It sometimes indicates instruction of a person to accept whatever is being said without assessing it critically. By indoctrination in the present paragraph we mean still more, the instilling of *false* teaching into the minds of the vulnerable. True instruction in the things of God is not indoctrination, but a desirable practice urged in Scripture. See the important passage Deuteronomy 6:4-25. In the first seven verses of Paul's second letter to Timothy the Holy Spirit obviously approves the Christian upbringing of Timothy from his earliest days.

Indoctrination in our third sense surfaces in traditional Roman Catholicism, where a special effort is made to gain the allegiance of the child at a very early age. Chinese Marxism insists that no one instruct a child in anything but 'suitable' doctrines until the age of eighteen years. Islamic society deliberately sets the child's mind and heart against Christianity by endless repetition of the catch-phrase that there is no god but Allah, and Mohammed is his prophet.

ZODIACAL ASTROLOGY

An earlier edition of the *Encyclopedia Britannica* defines astrology as 'the ancient art or science of divining the fate and future of human beings from indications given by the positions of the stars and other heavenly bodies'. The astrologer says that he or she can predict a person's destiny from a knowledge of the appearance of the sky at the time of birth. The Zodiac is a ring of twelve constellations above the earth's equator; actually an arbitrary band based on ancient ideas of what the patterns of stars look like. The stars are there, of course, but the interpretation comes from the viewers' minds!

Astrology is unbiblical, unscientific, and untrue — three descriptions that all mean the same thing. The Scriptures refer to astrology in both Testaments, always in a disapproving way (see 2 Kings 23:5, Isaiah 47:13, Daniel 2:2 and Acts 7:42,43). In fact, 'disapproving' is too mild a word, since the references show that God's judgment falls on astrologers and their works. The early Church would have nothing to do with astrology, though in the medieval period it crept back into a degenerate church. Some of the more liberal modern Biblical translators want the 'wise men' in Matthew 2 to be astrologers, but others carefully avoid an identification. God *approves* of the actions of the wise men, but *condemns* astrologers. They are therefore different.

INDEX

Anthroposophy 23

Armstrong, see Worldwide Church of God

Astrology 43

Bahaism 34, 37

British Israelites 37

Buddhism 16, 22, 37

Chinese Marxism 42

Christadelphians 14, 32

Christian Research Journal 25

Christian Scientists 11, 14, 31

Divine Light Mission 27, 38

Freemasonry 18, 22, 29, 32

Hare Krishna 38

Hinduism 16, 20, 22, 24, 34, 37, 38, 41

Islam 28, 38, 41, 42

Jehovah's Witnesses 11, 14, 22, 26, 32, 36, 40

Moonies 12, 16, 27, 29

Moral Re-Armament 15

Mormons 12, 18, 26, 28, 32, 40

New Age Movement 18, 34

New Apostolic Church 11, 25, 33, 40

Protestant Liberal 12, 13

Roman Catholicism 42

Satanists 20

Scientology 16, 29

Seventh Day Adventists 30, 36
Spiritism 20, 34
Swedenborg 18
Theosophy 18, 23, 27, 34
Transcendental Meditation 20, 38
Unity School of Christianity 14, 31
Worldwide Church of God 25, 32, 40
Yoga 20

Bryan Williams is the principal of the Bible Institute of South Africa, a theological college near Cape Town.

The author was born and brought up in New Zealand, where he attended Nelson College before training and qualifying as a pharmacist. In 1958 Bryan moved to the United Kingdom to study at London Bible College. He gained the BD of the University of London, and later completed a PhD with the Universities of Cape Town and Stellenbosch.

The Williams family – Bryan and Barbara, together with their son David and daughter Catherine – sailed to Cape Town twenty-five years ago in answer to an invitation to lecture at the Bible Institute. They have remained there ever since in spite of some attractive calls to positions in other parts of the world!

Bryan has written a number of articles and booklets. Other forms of Christian ministry include membership of South African missionary councils, preaching, and leadership positions in a local evangelical church. His hobbies are reading, photography and astronomy.

He has written *One Bible, One Message* (Common Mistakes About the Bible) and *What is Truth?* (an outline of the Christian Faith), both published by Evangelical Press of Wales.